Environn

Lifestyle Guide

For Grade 12 Students

VOL.10 OF 11

Financial

Jahangir Asadi

Vancouver, BC CANADA

Published by: Silosa Consulting Group Inc.
Vancouver, BC **CANADA**
Email: Info@Silosa.ca
www.silosa.ca

Ordering Information:
Quantity sales. Special discounts are available on quantity purchases by universities, schools, corporations, associations, and others. For details, contact the "Sales Department" at the above mentioned email address.

Environmental lifestyle Guide Vol.10 for Grade.12/J.Asadi —1st ed.
ISBN: 978-1-990451-84-3

Contents

We hope that, 10,000 years from now, future generations will be able to see flowers that provide bees with nectar and pollen and...
BEES provide flowers with the means to reproduce by spreading pollen from flower to flower,....

Jahangir Asadi

This book is dedicated to my professor, Dr.Bijan Esfandiari

Introduction

This book is part of an eleven volume series that is meant to be a standard textbook series, for grades 9 to 12. TTAIN & ESFK & SCG improves quality of life and reduces environmental degradation by fostering new consumption patterns and sustainable lifestyles through International Cooperative Extension Service programs at houses, offices, schools and libraries all over the globe.

Climate change is real. Therefore people have the potential to make a difference now and for future generations. This book provides climate science basics, including the roles that lifestyles and populations play in the climate scenario, the significance of carbon footprints, and an overview of the current climate situation. The manual has been categorized based on humanity's needs starting first with food and ending with tourism. The manual then illustrates the difference between adaptation (taking steps to live with the changes) and mitigation (taking steps to slow the rate of change.)

Adaptation examples include food, energy, transportation, recreation. Mitigation focuses on effectively engaging with local governments, through serving on advisory boards, communicating with public officials, educational institutes, schools, universities, libraries and leading communities towards climate change actions.

One useful way to mitigate climate change is through increasing public knowledge to better understand the impact of the rate of change on plants and animals. This is crucial for preserving species; and for assessing potential insects and disease outbreaks in agriculture, natural resources and public health.

Taking personal action is a key element of this manual.

Citizens are challenged to consume 20% fewer resources, to bring world consumption levels down as much as possible. Readers are given 12 practical steps to take to make the changes. The resources section provides additional information, and readers are encouraged to contact the author for further questions.

As an accessibility action, we have provided Online international courses on climate change control as well. You can access the courses via the following link:

http://TopTenAward.org

SILOSA Consulting Group (SCG)

Silosa Consulting Group (SCG) was established to provide outstanding consulting services of management system & educational standards to individuals, groups, companies, schools, and organizations all over the globe. SCG is publishing an "Environmental Lifestyle Guide " book series as a standard textbook related to increasing environmental awareness of students means being aware of the natural environment and making choices that benefit the earth, rather than hurt it. Vol.1 to 11 (for grades 9 to 12) providing some of the ways to practice environmental awareness include: **Recycling**, **Conserving energy and water**, **Reuse, Activism, and others**.

SCG book publishing services and distribution services are connected to over 39,000 booksellers worldwide, including Apple, Amazon, Barnes & Noble, Indigo, Google Play Books, and many more. SCG has enough experiences to help create new and effective environmental educational programmes in different countries all over the world. For more detail, visit our website : http://silosa.ca and/or send your enquirer to the following email:

info@silosa.ca

CHAPTER 1

About ISO 14000 for Students

The International Organization for Standardization is an independent, non-governmental organization, the members of which are the standards organizations of the 165 member countries. It is the world's largest developer of voluntary international standards and it facilitates world trade by providing common standards among nations. More than twenty thousand standards have been set, covering everything from manufactured products and technology to food safety, agriculture, and healthcare.

Kids ISO 14000s
"Kids ISO 14000s" is a new environmental education program for children, based on ISO 14000s, which is international standard for environmental management. Primary aims of this program are: -
1. To teach and train children how to manage the environmental issues (such as energy saving) by themselves through the working book and guide book of this program,
2. To certify those children who showed good accomplishment in the program from highly international authority (as is the case of ISO 14000s)
3. To network those children through the international network (Kids International Network), so that the children can work on the environment, internationally.

2. System of Kids ISO 14000s Program
The system of Kids ISO 14000s Program consists of
1. Operation Headquarter (ArTech).
2. Workbook, Guidebook (originally published by ArTech, and local versions are produced by each countries).
3. Eco-Kids-Instructors for local operation and evaluation of the performance of the children.
4. International accreditation committee for accreditation of accomplishment of the children, for certification of the Eco-Kids-Instructors, as well as overall checks of this program.
5. Linkage with international organizations (such as UNU, UNESCO, etc. …) And also national organizations

More information can be obtained :

www.ISO.org

Canada

Environmental Sustain for Future kids established in Vancouver, BC Canada in 2020. (ESFK) is an international ecolabel focused on taking care of environment for future of kids. ESFK defined as 'self-declared' environmental claims made by manufacturers and businesses based on ISO 14020 series of standards, the claimant can declare the environmental objectives and targets in relation to taking care of environment for future kids. However, this declaration will be verifiable.

Environmental Sustain for Future Kids
Vancouver, BC CANADA

Email: info@esfk.org
Web: www.esfk.org

STEP TEN

All about 'Eco-friendly'
Financial Products and/or Services

Green loans, energy efficiency mortgages, alternative energy venture capital, eco-savings deposits, and "green" credit cards; these items represent merely a handful of innovative, "green" financial products that are currently offered around the globe1 . In an age where environmental risks and opportunities abound, so too have the options for reconciling environmental matters with lending and financing arrangements.

The purpose of this Volume is to examine the currently available Eco friendly financial products and services, with a focus on lesson learning opportunities, the nature and transferability of best practices, and how key designs can potentially increase market share and generate profits, while improving brand recognition and enhancing reputation.

In this volume we have divides the financial services sector into the following categories:

1) Green Retail Banking;
2) Green Corporate and Investment Banking;
3) Insurance
4) Asset Management;

1. Green Retail Banking

Retail banking covers personal and business banking products and services designed for individuals, households and SMEs, rather than large corporate or institutional clients. Products and services in the eco friendly retail space include Green loans and mortgages, debit and credit card services, travelers' cheques, money orders, overdraft protection, cash management services and insurance, among others.

2. Green Corporate and Investment Banking

Corporate and investment banking, or "wholesale banking", sees banks provide banking solutions to large corporations, institutions, governments and other public entities with complex financial needs, typically international in scope. Financial institutions offering corporate and investment banking can underwrite debt issues, both on their own behalf and for corporate and public sector clients, as well as supply equity, manage funds and offer advice to corporate mergers and acquisitions. These banks act as financial intermediaries, raising capital (equity and debt) by trading foreign exchange, commodities and equity securities on the primary market.

3) Insurance

The insurance sector can generally be divided into two categories:
Life Insurance; and General (Non-Life) Insurance.
"Green" insurance falls under the latter and typically encompasses two product areas:
1) those which allow an insurance premium differentiation on the basis of environmentally relevant characteristics; and
2) Insurance products specifically tailored for clean technologies and emissions reducing activities.

4) Asset Management

Asset Management has become one of the fastest growing segments in the financial industry and represents a core business unit of current banks. This space focuses on providing financial advice to clients on estate planning, mutual funds, managed asset programs, taxes, trust services, international financial planning, global private banking and full-service and discount brokerages.

Green Retail Banking

Ask something more from your local Bank

 Home Mortgage	• 'green' mortgage initiative. %1 reduction on interest • for loans that meet environmental criteria. • Free home energy rating and offsets carbon emissions for every year of loan • Green Power Oriented Mortgage • 10% premium refund on its mortgage loan insurance
 Commercial Building Loan	• Green Loans for new condos • Developers do not have to pay an initial premium for "green" commercial buildings • Provides 1/8 of 1% discount on loans to green leadership projects
 Auto Loan	Clean Air Auto Loan with preferential rates for hybrids & Electrical
 Credit Card	Climate Credit Card. Bank will donate to WWF GreenCard Visa is the world's first credit card to offer an emissions offset program
 Deposit	Fully-insured deposits earmarked for lending to local energy-efficient companies aiming to reduce waste/pollution, or conserve natural resources

Green Corporate and Investment Banking

Ask something more from your local Bank

 Project Finance	Specialized service divisions are dedicated to long-term financing of clean energy projects. Some banks also specialize in one (or several) renewable technology type and/or place a premium on working with states where regulatory framework and government policy encourages the early adoption of clean technologies.
 Securitization	A risk sharing arrangement for environmental projects. Financial institution represents a guarantor (or structuring investor) at the mezzanine level of risk, allowing client to transfer risk to bank. Eco-Securitization scheme will test the feasibility of financing "natural infrastructure" by linking sustainable management of resources with the funding capacity and requirements of asset-backed securitization.
 Carbon Finance	Banks provide equity, loans and/or upfront or upon delivery payments to acquire carbon credits from projects. Most acquire carbon credits in order to serve their corporate clients' compliance needs, supply a tradable product to the banks' trading desks, or develop lending products backed by emission allowances and carbon credits.
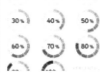 Indices	Series of environmental private investor eco-market products includes a biofuels commodity basket, total returns solar energy index, clean renewable energy index and total returns water index (e.g., enables interested parties to invest in water as a commodity).
 Deposit	Fully-insured deposits earmarked for lending to local energy-efficient companies aiming to reduce waste/pollution, or conserve natural resources

Insurance

Ask something more from your local Insurance Co.

 Auto Insurance	Pay As You Drive™ Insurance. Mileage-based Insurance. 10% discount for hybrid and fuel efficient vehicles. Bank can also choose to offset vehicle's annual emissions (e.g. 20 % emissions offset through Climate Care Recycling Insurance. Customer pays less for car insurance, by up to 20%, if recycled parts are used when vehicle is damaged and requires service.
 Building and Home Insurance	Green Building Replacement and Upgrade Coverage. Product covers unique type of "green" risks related to the sustainable building industry. "Climate Neutral" Home Insurance Policy. First home insurance product to carry out GHG offsetting based on customer usage.
 Business Insurance	Environmental Damage Insurance.

Asset Management

Ask something more from your local Financial Organization

 Fisacl Green Fund	By purchasing shares or investing in Green Funds, customers receive an income tax discount, and thus accept a lower interest rate on investment. Banks can offer loans at lower cost to finance environmental projects related to eligible categories.
 Fund	Eco Performance is the world's largest "green" fund. %80 of assets are channeled towards eco and social leaders, with %20 going to "eco-innovators". Equity Fund - Future Energy, focuses on clean energy sector investments in clean four energy-related business segments.
 Cat Bond Fund	Cat Bond Fund. World's first public fund for catastrophe bonds, a portion of which is aimed at climate-related natural disasters (or climate adaptation). Vehicle designed to hedge climate risks typically difficult to cover in the traditional insurance market.

Conclusion

Many "green" financial products and services, reviewed above, either remain in the nascent stage of development/implementation or data related to their success/failure has not yet been generated or reported.

Due to this lack of experience and data, any rigorous measurement or ranking of these designs would be overly speculative and risk misrepresenting some designs over others. Looking ahead, however, as more quantitative and qualitative track records emerge for these products,

The following questions should be considered when gauging product performance or promise:

- Does it achieve high levels of financial performance?
- Does it attract a particularly large number of customers?
- Does it last over time, and is re-launched year by year?
- Does it raise the environmental awareness among all stakeholders, including clients and employees?
- Does it receive positive attention from the media and environmental NGOs?
- Does it prompt the introduction of other environmental products and services?
- Does it improve brand recognition and corporate image among stakeholders?

As environmental understanding and awareness grows in North America, so too will the demand for products and services aimed at facilitating the advancement of environmentally sustainable lives, livelihoods and communities. At the same time, this demand will also expose new business opportunities, while leading to an increased diversification of products and services found in multiple sectors. Consequently, organizations that have the foresight and capacity to tap into this desire by consumers to affect positive environmental change will likely experience widespread benefits; from improved corporate image to increased growth and competitiveness in the marketplace. Given their intermediary role in the economy and farreaching customer base, financial institutions will be well-positioned to reap financial and non-financial rewards, while furthering their contribution toward sustainable development.

Are Crypto Currencies Inherently Bad For The Environment?
All cryptocurrencies have an energy and environmental problem. But if done right, it might be possible to channel all that energy into something good for the planet.

Crypto's environmental troubles

A fierce debate around the environmental impacts of cryptocurrencies, like bitcoin, is growing. Bitcoin does consume a lot of energy. That energy use is growing and annually consumes as much energy as whole nations, such as Finland, Malaysia, or Sweden. While bitcoin is not the only industry to consume as much energy as entire countries, e.g. concrete consumes more energy than India, the energy both sectors consume comes with associated pollution, including carbon emissions.

Even transactions with bitcoin use a lot of energy, with the average transaction consuming over 1,700 kWh of electricity, which is almost twice the monthly amount used by the average U.S. home. However, there was ways to transact in bitcoin using much less energy.

Exacerbating this problem, some bitcoin mining operations have teamed up with struggling fossil fuel power plants, keeping some power plants online that would otherwise have retired, increasing overall carbon emissions. Some utilities have even gotten into the bitcoin game directly.

Large bitcoin mining operations are also moving locations as China, the country previously with the largest bitcoin mining industry, recently banned both cryptocurrency mining and transactions. This change has bitcoin mining operations moving to places like Texas and potentially Alberta, Canada.

All else equal, bitcoin operations that co-locate and utilize fossil fuels that would have otherwise stayed in the ground will increase emissions.

Some are considering using stranded natural gas that would otherwise have been flared, which, absent any methane venting and flaring regulations, would make the use of the natural gas for bitcoin, at-best, carbon neutral. However, it is a stretch, and making the natural gas more valuable at the wellhead could further dissuade pipeline development that would have moved the gas to market.

However, co-locating bitcoin mining operations with zero-carbon resources, such as nuclear, hydro, wind and solar, could help reduce the carbon emissions associated with the mining itself. Co-location could also give a financial boost to power plants that might be able to sell their electricity at a higher price to miners instead of to the grid when demand and prices are low. This type of hybrid power plant/mine might even make uneconomical projects economical.

Going further, it is also possible that the cryptocurrency mines themselves could offer benefits directly to the grid, and, if operated intelligently, even result in lower overall carbon emissions.

A positive grid impact?

The study simulated the evolution of the Electric Reliability Council of Texas (ERCOT), the grid that serves most of Texas, out to 2030 under multiple scenarios:
1) a base case with no datacenter/bitcoin mining expansion,
2) a case with 5 GW of inflexible (always on) datacenter/bitcoin mines by 2030,
3) a scenario with 5 GW of mildly flexible datacenters deployed by 2030 and
4) a scenario with 5 GW of very flexible datacenters deployed by 2030.

The non-flexible scenario added a significant baseload to the ERCOT system. This growth resulted in the deployment of more power plant capacity that the base case, including more wind, natural gas, and solar.

This increased energy use also resulted in an additional 7.9 million metric tons of carbon emissions over the base case by 2030.

However, the flexible scenarios were more interesting. Both flexible scenarios actually see more wind and less natural gas deployed than both the base case and the inflexible scenarios.

This change is because the datacenters/mines were programed to reduce their energy consumption by certain percentages when electricity prices hit certain tiers. In total, the third scenario saw the datacenters/mines curtailing their load about 14% of the year.

The flexibility of the datacenters/mines in the latter two scenarios allowed the model to deploy different levels of technologies than the base or inflexible case. The model actually built more renewables because it could utilize the flexibility of the datacenters/mines to compensate for fluctuations in renewable output. This flexibility also resulted in lower carbon emissions compared to the base case.

For additional load to result in lower total carbon emissions, the additional energy consumption must be offset by more zero-carbon energy. In the flexible datacenter/mine cases, the amount of energy generated from wind and solar was more than in the base case and the amount generated from natural gas was lower.

In general, the flexibility of the datacenters/mines moves their load to more value energy over power, which better aligns with renewables. This is because renewables are great at providing large amounts of energy, but have less ability to always provide capacity, or constant power.

In concept, flexible datacenters/mines are similar to the electrification of transportation or heating with the ability to control then times when the chargers and heaters operate. However, it is likely that datacenters/mines could offer large levels of flexible load concentrated in a smaller number of locations, which could make their administration easier.

Grid decarbonization studies often assume high levels of flexible demand, and often much of this flexibility comes from diffuse sources, such as smart thermostats and EV charging. While this analysis did not seek to satisfy any carbon policy, it does illustrate the potential carbon benefits of high levels of flexible demand coupled with an electricity market that is able to incorporate it.

Mining and transacting cryptocurrencies, such as bitcoin, do present energy and emissions challenges, but new research shows that there are possible pathways to mitigate some of these issues if cryptocurrency miners are willing to operate in a way to compliment the deployment of more low-carbon energy.

The author of this Book does not currently own or mine any cryptocurrencies.

1) Green Retail Banking, Ask something more from your local Bank, green mortgage initiative. 1% reduction on interest, for loans that meet environmental criteria
A) True
B) False
ANSWER:

2) Clean Air Auto Loan with preferential rates for hybrids & Electrical
A) True
B) False
ANSWER:

3) What is Climate Credit Card. Bank will donate to WWF
A) True
B) False
ANSWER:

4) Even transactions with _____ use a lot of energy, with the average transaction and is not environmentally.
A) credit card
B) bitcoin
C) debit card
D) All of them
ANSWER:

5) Fully-insured deposits earmarked for lending to local energy-efficient companies aiming to reduce waste/ pollution, or conserve natural resources
A) True
B) False
ANSWER:

6) Specialized service divisions are dedicated to long-term financing of clean energy projects.
A) True
B) False
ANSWER:

7) Insurance, Pay as You Drive™ Insurance. Mileage-based Insurance, __ discount for hybrid and fuel efficient vehicles.
A) %5
B) %10
C) %15
D) %7
ANSWER:

8) Many "green" financial products and services, reviewed above, either remain in the nascent stage of development/implementation or data related to their success/failure has not yet been generated or reported.
A) True
B) False
ANSWER:

9) Provides 8/1 of __ discount on loans to green leadership.
A) %5
B) %1
C) %15
D) %7
ANSWER:

10) Nine Percent of emissions offset through _____ _____ _____.
A) free home energy
B) reduction on interest
C) Climate Care Recycling
D) All of them
ANSWER:

11) All cryptocurrencies have an energy and environmental problem. But if done right, it might be possible to channel all that energy into something good for the planet.
A) True
B) False
ANSWER:

12) Insurance product to carry out _____ offsetting based on.
A) COD
B) BOD
C) CCC
D) GHG
ANSWER:

13) Who does consume a lot of energy?
A) credit card
B) bitcoin
C) debit card
D) All of them
ANSWER:

14) Seventy percent emissions offset through Climate Care Recycling.
A) True
B) False
ANSWER:

15) Been flared, which, absent any methane venting and flaring regulations, would make the use of the natural gas for bitcoin, at-best, carbon neutral.
A) True
B) False
ANSWER:

16) Fisacl Green Fund. By purchasing shares or investing in _____
Funds, customers receive an income tax discount, and thus.
A) credit card
B) special
C) green
D) All of them
ANSWER:

17) Ask something more green and environmental programs from
your local Bank.
A) True
B) False
ANSWER:

18) Bitcoin use a lot of energy, with the average transaction
consuming over 1,700 kWh of electricity, which is almost twice the
monthly amount used by the average U.S. home.
A) 1,100 kWh
B) 1,000 kWh
C) 1,700 kWh
D) 1,500 kWh
ANSWER:

19) This growth resulted in the deployment of more power plant
capacity that the base case, including more wind, natural gas, and
solar. This increased energy use also resulted in an additional 7.9
million metric tons of carbon emissions over the base case by _____.
A)2030
B)2040
C)2050
D)2020
ANSWER:

20) Eighty Percent of assets are channeled towards eco and social.
 A) True
 B) False
ANSWER:

21) What are some other examples of products and services offered by Green Corporate and Investment Banking?
A) Green loans and mortgages
B) debit and credit card services
C) travelers› cheques, money orders
D) All of them
ANSWER:

Bibliography:

Amberg, N.; Magda, R. Environmental Pollution and Sustainability or the Impact of the Environmentally Conscious Measures of International Cosmetic Companies on Purchasing Organic Cosmetics. Visegrad J. Bioecon. Sustain. Dev. 2018, 1, 23.

Asadi, J., "International Environmental Labelling, Economic Consequencies, Export Magazine, July 2001

Asadi, J. 2008. Mobile Phone as management systems tools, ISO Magazine, Vol.8, No.1

Asadi, J., Eco-Labelling Standards, National Standard Magazine, Sep. 2004.

Barbieux, D.; Padula, A.D. Paths and Challenges of New Technologies: The Case of Nanotechnology-Based Cosmetics Development in Brazil. Adm. Sci. 2018, 8, 16.

Advanced Engineering and Applied Sciences: An International Journal 2014; 4(3): 26-28

Berolzheimer, C. (2006). Pencils: An Environmental Profile.

Chemical Week, 1999. Europe's Beef Ban Tests Precautionary Principle. (August 11).

Chaudri, S.K.; Jain, N.K. History of Cosmetics. Asian J. Pharm. 2009, 7–9, 164–167.

CHOI, J.P. Brand Extension as Informational Leverage. Review of Eco- nomic Studies, Vol. 65 (1998), pp. 655-669.

Conway, G. 2000. Genetically modified crops: risks and promise.

Corrado, M., (1989), The Greening Consumer in Britain, MORI, London

Corrado, M., (1997), Green Behaviour – Sustainable Trends, Sustainable Lives?, MORI, london, accessed via countries. Manila, Asian Development Bank 33p.

Davies, Clive. Chief, Design for the Environment Program, Environmental Protection Agency. Interview. March 24, 2009.

Federal Trade Commission, "Sorting Out Green Advertising Claims." http://www.ftc.gov/bcp/edu/pubs/consumer/general/gen02.shtm (March 26, 2009, March 27, 2009)

Ooyen, Carla. Research Manager with Nutrition Business Journal. Personal correspondence. March 19, 2009.

Tekin, Jenn. Marketing Manager with Packaged Facts & SBI. Personal correspondence. March 17, 2009.

University of California - Berkeley. http://berkeley.edu/news/media/releases/2006/05/22_householdchemicals.shtml (March 26, 2009)

U.S. Department of Health and Human Services, Household Products Database.http://householdproducts.nlm.nih.gov/cgi-bin/household/prodtree?prodcat=Inside+the+Home (March 17,

Women's Voices of the Earth, "Household Cleaning Products and Effects on Human Health."http://www.womenandenvironment.org/campaignsandprograms/SafeCleaning/safecleaninghealth (March 17, 2009)

ISO 14020, ISO 14021,ISO 14024,ISO 14025, International Organization for Standardization.

Environmental Finance. 2007(a). In Brief: FTSE4Good Sets Out Climate Criteria. March.

Environmental Finance. 2007(b). Corporate Profile: New Resource Bank (NRB) - Making Their Green, Greener. February.

Environmental Finance. 2007 (c). ABN Amro Launches Climate Change Index. March 29. http://www.environmental-finance.com/onlinews/0329abn.htm

Environmental Finance. 2003. Are Cat Bonds Changing Course? http://www.environmental-finance.com/2003/0304apr/catbonds.htm

Esty, D. and A. Winston. 2006. Green to Gold: How Companies Use Environmental Strategy to Innovate, Create Value and Build Competitive Advantage. New Haven.

Current Trends and Future Opportunities in North America 51

ETA (Environmental Transportation Agency). 2007. Britain's First Climate Neutral Home Insurance to Offset Customers' Usage. Press Release. February 1. www.eta.co.uk

EuroMoney Institutional Investor, 2005. http://www.invenergyllc.com/

Fireman's Fund. 2007. Green-Gard Coverages. www.firemansfund.com

Funding Universe. Corporation History: MBNA. http://www.fundinguniverse.com

GreenBiz.com. 2006(a). New Resource Bank Announces Plan to Finance Residential Solar Systems. October 24. San Francisco. www.greenbiz.com

GreenBiz.com. 2006(b). Survey: Majority of Investment Managers Link Corporate Responsibility to Asset Performance.

Green Finance Products and Services, NATF Report, AUgust 2007

March 17. http://www.greenbiz.com/news/news_third.cfm?NewsID=30617

GreenBiz.com. 2004. Builders Break Ground on World's Most Environmentally Responsible High Rise Office Building. August 4. www.greenbiz.com

Greener Buildings. 2007. New Bank Aims to Make It Easier to Build Green. Produced by GreenBiz.com. February 1. http://www.greenbiz.com/sites/greenerbuildings/news_detail.cfm?NewsID=34525

GreenCard Visa. 2007. Netherlands. http://www.greencardvisa.nl/

Green Car Congress. 2007. Reported US Sales of Hybrids Up 26% in April. May 3. http://www.greencarcongress.com/2007/05/reported_us_sal.html

Grundon. 2005. Financial Close for Slough Energy from Waste Facility Announced by Lakeside Energy from Waste Ltd.News Bulletin. October 3. http://www.grundon.com

Harris, A. 2005. Supporting Climate Change Solutions. VanCity Presentation for Pollution Probe on Complementary

Mechanisms. June 28. www.pollutionprobe.org/Happening/pdfs/complementarymeas-June28/harris.pdf

IISD (International Institute for Sustainable Development). 2007. Business and Sustainable Development: A Global Guide. www.bsdglobal.com

Innis, R. 2006. A Theory of Consumer Boycotts under Symmetric Information and Imperfect Competition. Economic Journal. Vol. 116, issue 511, pg 355-381.

Institute for Market Transformation to Sustainability. 2005. Special Report: Green Mortgage-Backed Securities One Step Closer to Reality. Building Operating Management Magazine. December. http://www.facilitiesnet.com/bom/article.asp?id=3623

ISO (International Standards Organization). 1999. Financing Catastrophe Risk: Capital Market Solutions.. Studies and Analyses. http://www.iso.com/studies_analyses/hurricane_experience/financingrisk.html#14

Labatt, S. and R.W. White. 2007. Carbon Finance: The Financial Implications of Climate Change. John Wiley & Sons Inc.

Liu, Peter. Founder and CEO of New Resource Bank (NRB). Interview conducted in February 2007.

Joshua D. Rhodes, Ph.D., Is Bitcoin Inherently Bad For The Environment?

Jeucken, M. 2004. Sustainability in Finance: Banking on the Planet.

Jeucken, M. 2001. Sustainable Finance and Banking – Slow starters are gaining pace. Based on Jeucken's book Sustainable Finance and Banking. 2001. www.sustainability-in-finance.com

Kennedy, P.E. "Estimation with Correctly Interpreted Dummy Variables in Semilogarithmic Equations," American Economic Review 71: 801 (1981).

Kirchho®, S., (2000), Green Business and Blue Angels.

Kraus, Jeff. Lab Technician at the North Carolina School of Textiles.

Labeling Issues, Policies and Practices Worldwide.

Lamport, L. 1998. The cast of (timber) certifiers: who are they? International J. Ecoforestry 11(4): 118-122.

Large Scale impoverishment of Amazonian forests by logging and fire. 1999.

Lathrop, K.W. and Centner, T.J. 1998. Eco-labeling and ISO 14000: An analysis of US regulatory systems and issues concerning adoption of type II standards. Environmental

Lee, J. et al. 1996. Trade related environmental measures; sizing and comparing impacts.

Lehtonen, Markku. 1997. Criteria in Environmental Labeling: A comparative Analysis on Environmental Criteria in Selected Labeling Schemes. Geneva, UNEP. 148p.

LIEBI, T. Trusting Labels: A Matter of Numbers? Working Paper Uni versity of Bern, No. 0201 (2002).

Lindstrom, T. 1999. Forest Certification: The View from Europe's NIPFs. Journal of Forestry 97(3): 25-31. London

Losey, J.E., Rayor, L.S. & Carter, M.E. 1999. Transgenic pollen harms monarch larvae. Nature 399 20 May): p.214.

Mattel Ever After High Cedar Wood Doll. (2014, July 3).

Management 22 (2) : 163-172.

Mattoo, A. and H. V. Singh, (1994), Eco-Labelling: Policy Considera-Michaels, R. G., and V. K. Smith. "Market Segmentation And Valuing Amenities With Hedonic Models: The Case Of Hazardous Waste Sites," Journal of Urban Economics, 1990 28(2), 223-242.

Nicholson-Lord, D., (1993) 'Tis the Season to be Green, The Independent, 20 December

Nuttall, N., (1993), Shoppers can cross green products off their lists, The Times, 3 July

OCDE/GD(97)105. Paris, OECD. 81p.

OECD. "Ec-labelling: Actual Effects of Selected Programmes," OCDE/GD (97) 105, 1997, Paris. (available on line at http://www.oecd.org/env/eco/books.htm#trademono)

OECD. 1997a. Case study on eco-labeling schemes. Paris, OECD (30 Dec):

OECD. 1997b. Eco-labeling: Actual Effects of Selected Programs.

Osborne, L. "Market Structure, Hedonic Models, and the Valuation of Environmental Amenities." Unpublished Ph.D. dissertation. North Carolina State University, 1995.

Osborne, L., and V. K. Smith. "Environmental Amenities, Product Differentiation, and market Power," Mimeo, 1997.

Ozanne, L.K. and Vlosky, R.P. 1996. Wood products environmental certification: the United States perspective". Forestry Chronicle 72 (2) : 157-165.

Palmquist, R. B., F. M. Roka, and T.Vukina. "Hog Operations, Environmental Effects, and Residential Property Values," Land Economics 73(1), (1997): 114-24.

Palmquist, R.B. "Hedonic Methods," in J.B Braden and C.D. Kolstad, eds. Measuring the Demand for Environmental Improvement. Amsterdam, NL: Elsevier, 1991.

Paper Mate. (2014). Paper Mate Recycled.

Pento, T. 1997. Implementation of Public Green Procurement Programs (22-31) in Greener Purchasing: Opportunities and Innovations. Sheffield, Greenleaf Publ. 325 p.

Perloff, J. "Industrial Organization Lecture Notes," Mimeo. University of California at Berkeley (1985).

Plant, C. and Plant, J. 1991. Green business: hope or hoax? Philadelphia, New Society Publishers 136 p.

Pencil Making Today (2014, January 1). Pencil Making Today: How to Make a Pencil in 10 Steps.

Polak, J. and Bergholm, K. 1997. Eco-labeling and trade: a cooperative approach (Jan.): Policy in a Green Market. Environmental and Resource Economics 22, 419-

Poore, M.E.D. et al. 1989. No timber without trees. London, Earthscan. 352p.

Raff, D. M.G., and M. Trajtenberg. "Quality-Adjusted Prices for the American Automobile Industry: 1906-1940." NBER Working Paper Series, Working Paper No. 5035, February 1995.

Roberts, J. T. 1998. Emerging global environment standards: prospects and perils. Journal of Developing Societies 14 (1): 144-163.

Rosen, S., "Hedonic Prices and Implicit Markets: Product Differentiation in Pure Competition." Journal of Political Economy. 82: 34-55 (1974).

Ross, B. 1997. Eco-friendly procurement training course for UN HCR. : 126 p.

Ryan, S., and Skipworth, M., (1993), Consumers turn their backs on green revolution, The Times, 4 April

Salzman, J. 1997. Informing the Green Consumer: The Debate over the Use and Abuse of Environmental Labels. Journal of Industrial Ecology 1 (2): 11-22.

Sanders, W. 1997. Environmentally Preferable Purchasing: The US Experience (946-960) in Greener Purchasing: Opportunities and Innovations. Sheffield, Greenleaf Publ. 325p.

Sayre, D. 1996. Inside ISO 14000: The competitive advantage of environmental management. Delray Beach FL., St. Lucie Press. 232p.

Suzuki, D. (2014, January 1). PEG Compounds and their contaminants

SHAPIRO, C. Premiums for High Quality Products as Returns to Reputa- tion. Quarterly Journal of Economics, Vol. 98, No. 4 (1983), pp. 659-680.

Stillwell, M. and van Dyke, B. 1999. An activists handbook on genetically modified organisms and the WTO. Washington DC., The Consumer's Choice Council: 20 p.

Semenzato, A.; Costantini, A.; Meloni, M.; Maramaldi, G.; Meneghin, M.; Baratto, G. Formulating O/W Emulsions with Plant-Based Actives: A Stability Challenge for an Eective Product. Cosmetics 2018, 5, 59.

Sources of Plastics (2014, January 1). Sources of Plastics.

Singh, S. (2008, March 6). Paraffin wax.

Saint Jean Carbon. (n.d.). Sri Lankan Graphite.

Teisl, M. F., B. Roe, and R. L. Hicks. "Can Eco-labels tune a market? Evidence from dolphin-safe labeling," Presented paper at the 1997 American Agricultural Economics Association Meetings, Toronto.

Tollefson, Jennifer E. (2008). Calocedrus Decurrens.

THE GERSEN, C. Psychological Determinants of Paying Attention to Eco- Labels in Purchase Decisions: Model Development and Multinational Vali- dation. Journal of Consumer Policy, Vol. 23, No. 4 (2000), pp. 285-313.

Tibor, T. and Feldman, I. 1995. ISO 14000: a guide to the new environmental management standards. Burr Ridge Ill., Irwin Professional Publ. 250 p.

TU.S. Energy Information Administration, What is U.S. Electricity Generation by Energy Source?, Retrieved From: https://www.eia.gov/tools/faqs/faq.php?id=427&t=3

U.S. Energy Information Administration, Biomass Explained, Retrieved From: https://www.eia.gov/energyexplained/?page=biomass_home

U.S. Environmental Protection Agency. National Water Quality Fact Inventory: 1990 Report to Congress. EPA 503-9-92-006, Apr. 1992.

UK Eco-labelling Board website, accessed via http://www.ecosite.co.uk/Ecolabel-UK/

US Environmental Protection Agency (EPA742-R-99-001): 40 p. <www.epa.gov/opptintr/epp>

US EPA, 1993. Determinants of effectiveness for environmental certification and labeling programs. Washington, D.C., US Environmental Protect

US EPA, 1993. Status report on the use of environmental labels worldwide. Washington, D.C., US Environmental Protection Agency (742-R-93-001 September).

US EPA, 1993. The use of life-cycle assessment in environmental labeling. Washington, D.C., US Environmental Protection Agency (742-R-93-003 September).

US EPA, 1998. Environmental labeling: issues, policies, and practices worldwide. Washington DC., Environmental Protection Agency, Pollution Prevention Division Prepared by Abt

US EPA, 1999. Comprehensive procurement guidelines (CPG) program. Washington, D.C., US Environmental Protection Agency: <www.epa.gov/cpg>

US EPA, 1999. Environmentally preferable purchasing program: Private sector pioneers: How companies are incorporating environmentally preferable purchases. Washington University of Saskatchewan, Sustainable purchasing guide.

USG, 1993. Federal acquisition, recycling, and waste prevention. Washington DC., Executive Order: (20 October).

USG, 1998. Greening the government through waste prevention, recycling, and federal acquisition. Washington, D.C., Executive Order 13101 (September).

Kijjoa, A.; Sawangwong, P. Drugs and Cosmetics from the Sea. Mar. Drugs 2004, 2, 73–82. [CrossRef]

Wang, J.; Pan, L.; Wu, S.; Lu, L.; Xu, Y.; Zhu, Y.; Guo, M.; Zhuang, S. Recent Advances on Endocrine Disrupting Eects of UV Filters. Int. J. Environ. Res. Public Health 2016, 13, 782.

Bilal, A.I.; Tilahun, Z.; Shimels, T.; Gelan, Y.B.; Osman, E.D. Cosmetics Utilization Practice in Jigjiga Town, Eastern Ethiopia: A Community Based Cross-Sectional Study. Cosmetics 2016, 3, 40.

Ting, C.T.; Hsieh, C.M.; Chang, H.-P.; Chen, H.-S. Environmental Consciousness and Green Customer Behavior: The Moderating Roles of Incentive Mechanisms. Sustainability 2019, 11, 819.

Chen, K.; Deng, T. Research on the Green Purchase Intentions from the Perspective of Product Knowledge. Sustainability 2016, 8, 943.

Wang, H.; Ma, B.; Bai, R. How Does Green Product Knowledge Eectively Promote Green Purchase Intention? Sustainability 2019, 11, 1193.

Nguyen, T.T.H.; Yang, Z.; Nguyen, N.; Johnson, L.W.; Cao, T.K. Greenwash and Green Purchase Intention: The Mediating Role of Green Skepticism. Sustainability 2019, 11, 2653.

Cinelli, P.; Coltelli, M.B.; Signori, F.; Morganti, P.; Lazzeri, A. Cosmetic Packaging to Save the Environment: Future Perspectives. Cosmetics 2019, 6, 26.

Eixarch, H.; Wyness, L.; Siband, M. The Regulation of Personalized Cosmetics in the EU. Cosmetics 2019, 6, 29.

CANADA SILVER BEAVER BADGE

Participate in our Online Classes to earn these exclusive digital badges!
www.toptenaward.org

Design & Development by:

Tara Asadi

CANADA BRONZE BEAVER BADGE

Participate in our Online Classes to earn these exclusive digital badges!
www.toptenaward.org

Design & Development by:

Tara Asadi

CANADA GOLD BEAVER BADGE

Participate in our Online Classes to earn these exclusive digital badges!

Design & Development by:

Tara Asadi

Environmental Lifestyle Guide

For Grade 9

For Grade 10

**Plus Online Certification Tests via:
https://toptenaward.org**

Standard Text Books

For Grade 11

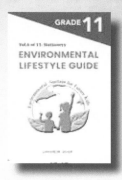  

For Grade 12

**Environmental Lifestyle Guide
Standard Text Book**
For Students Grade 9 to 12
Available in more than
39,000 Bookstores
all over the globe.
https://ecofriendlyeducation.com

Cooperation by:
Top Ten Award International Network
&
Environmental Sustain for Future Kids

Lightning Source UK Ltd.
Milton Keynes UK
UKHW050515120123
415202UK00001B/5

9 7 8 1 9 9 0 4 5 1 8 4 3